I spent last year
talking to the wild...

and this is what the
wild replied

What the Wild Replied

POEMS FROM
HUMAN NATURE

Becky Hemsley

WILDMARK

PUBLISHING

Becky Hemsley at Wildmark Publishing

COVER DESIGN BY LERAYNNE
leraynne.myportfolio.com

EMAIL ENQUIRIES: info@talkingtothewild.com

ISBN 978-1-7398245-3-2

For Avril

keep dancing up there Mrs C

xxx

I have always been drawn to nature. So much of my writing is inspired by the synchronicity I see between nature out in the world and our human nature within. We all have our sunny days and our storms. We all know what it's like for things to feel a little dark and we enjoy those times when things feel light and bright. We grow, we rest, we let go and we reap what we sow. Just as the world around us does.

And this got me thinking about the idea that human beings have their own seasons. This doesn't mean that our seasons correspond with those of the natural world. For example, Autumn is my favourite season. It is when I am usually my most creative, my most authentic and my most comfortable. It is the season when things tend to come to fruition in my life. In that sense, it is probably more like my own personal summer.

The idea that we have seasons though, is something I wanted to really explore, and the more I thought about it, the more it made sense. Our lives tend to be cyclical. We grow and we learn and then we go through a period of enjoying where that takes us. Then we realise there are things in our lives that are not serving us and so we let go, reassess and take some time to figure things out. When we let go, we have to process the loss and we tend to find this difficult, even if we knew it was for the best. But once we have made our peace with it, we are ready for the cycle to begin again. Less like a never-ending circle but more like a spiral I suppose – we are always climbing slightly higher up the spiral with each period of growth and learning.

With this in mind, I've decided to divide the poems in this book into the four seasons. Again, this does not mean that the poems in the 'Winter' section will refer to winter in the natural world, but more your own personal winter. The times when you feel a little lost and overwhelmed and life can feel a bit bleak. And it doesn't mean that we don't have days or periods of 'winter' in the other seasons. Here in the UK, it is not unusual for a day in October for example, to tease us with elements of summer, spring and autumn all in one. And the same is true for all of us. We can be in the middle of our own summer and still have a day or two of rain.

So, dip in and out as you need to with this book. You may find poems that, for you personally, apply far more to a different season than the one I have assigned it to. There will always be overlap. I have started with winter because, here in the UK, it is the season we start the year with and because I didn't want to end the book on a season that could feel a little heavy.

What I would stress however, is that winter doesn't need to feel dark and cold all the time. We need those periods of rest, processing and darkness in order to emerge ready to grow. So, whilst many of the poems in 'Winter' may seem a little oppressive, I hope that there are moments of hope and light in there too.

After my first book, I started posting and reciting many of my poems on social media and I began to get requests for topics to write about. Some have been quite general (a poem about navigating the teenage years for example) and some were very specific. Where there have been specific requests, I have included a note before the poems as they appear in this book. Whilst general poems tend to be more self-explanatory (you'll know the teenage years poem as soon as you read it), others could be a little confusing without context, hence the explanations.

I am always happy to take requests! It often challenges me to think outside the box or to do research about things I have not experienced - and I consider that to be only a positive thing. I still have a list of requests that I am trying to work my way through, but if there is anything in particular you would like to hear from me, you can find – and contact – me at the following places:

Email: info@beckyhemsley.com
Facebook: Becky Hemsley – Talking to the Wild
Instagram: @talkingtothewild
Tik Tok: @talkingtothewild
Twitter: @talking2wild
Pinterest: Becky Hemsley
Etsy Shop: Talking to the Wild

As I said in my first book, I use a mixture of pronouns and voices in my poems. My hope is that the message of each individual poem still talks to you, regardless of which pronoun/voice is used.

I also mentioned in my first book that I rhyme/half rhyme my poems based on my own accent. I have become more conscious of this and have adapted at times to try and make the poems rhyme for all. However, there have been a few times I've not been able to do that. I also use the spellings that we use here in the UK which can sometimes differ slightly from what some readers are used to (e.g realise vs realize and colour vs color). Again, I hope you can still hear the message regardless.   xxx

CONTENTS

WINTER

storms, cold, bleakness,
darkness, persevering,
challenges, resting, grief

BATTLE

when life feels like a battle
in the middle of a war
and your battle cry's a whisper
'cause your voice has lost its roar

when the shield that you carry
can't protect you like it should
and you're struggling to fire your arrows
like you normally would

when your armour weighs you down,
you are battered and you're bruised
when the enemy's advancing
and you're sure you're going to lose

when battle feels exhausting,
put down your sword and rest
save your energy because
the war's not over yet

but also look around you
to the others in the fray
and listen for the army
that is calling out your name

tell them you are wounded
that you stumbled and you fell
because, beneath your armour
there's a chance they cannot tell

let them cover you
say you will do the same for them
when they are hurt and wounded
and your strength returns again

for now, retreat a little
from the weariness of war
but remember you've survived
each battle you have fought before

so give yourself some credit
'cause you've made it all this way
and I promise you are strong enough
to fight another day

THE CLIMB

they say that when you're broken
this is how the light gets in
but what if all the cracks
are letting out the light within?

they say it makes you stronger
but at first it makes you weak
the way you face the mountain base
before you climb its peak

they say to break is brave
and yet your mind is full of dread
you're not overwhelmed by courage
but by helplessness instead

but admitting you are breaking
is far braver than you know
and remember, from the bottom
there is just one way to go

see I think they mean it isn't just
that breaking makes you strong
but the way you use the embers
of your will to carry on

it's triumph over trauma
and it's healing after hurt
it's rising from the ashes
with a new-found sense of worth

so find yourself a candle
and allow its tiny spark
to ignite you back to life
and put the fire back in your heart

and grant yourself compassion
for the times that you feel weak
just rest until you're strong enough
to get back on your feet

yes, I know that when you're broken
you have only threads of hope
but tie them to the mountain
like your personal safety rope

then gather at the bottom
with the summit high above
and take a breath, then take a step
the only way is up

REQUEST:

Anxiety/worry

THE CASTLE WALLS

you brace yourself for battle
for the soon-approaching war
and the sky echoes your darkness
as grey clouds begin to form

you retreat inside your castle
where the walls are tall and strong
but in the darkness, the walls whisper
of all the things that could go wrong

so you run around your castle
closing curtains, locking doors
and you batten down your hatches
in preparation for the storm

but locked inside your keep
you miss the sky return to blue
and behind the doors and curtains
you can't see the stunning view

see the castle's kept you listening
to all the words it's said
whilst the storm outside has passed
as you've raged war inside your head

but remember, it's your castle
and the walls belong to you
so don't let them try to tell you
what you can and cannot do

refuse to lose your voice to theirs
and do not let them speak
for they'll never give up trying
to convince you that you're weak

wrap a robe of strength around you
wear your courage like a crown
and you'll silence all the whispers
that have tried to talk you down

and if you find yourself in battle,
use your fortress by all means
but remember – you are in control
yes, it's a castle...

but you're the Queen

CRYING OUT LOUD

they handed her the baby
and he roared a deafening cry
with tears of raw emotion
that announced his start to life

they knew that he was breathing
for his lungs to make that sound
and they knew that he was telling them
that life felt upside down

they knew he had the instinct
to reach out to someone else
that he longed to rest in someone's arms
just knowing it would help

but they didn't try and stop him,
didn't tell him he was weak
they simply gave him comfort
when they knew he couldn't speak

so next time you feel something
that you can't put into words,
when life feels overwhelming,
you need comfort from this world

just let it out – you're human
and those tears that fall are proof
that crying out for help
is the most natural thing to do

and seek out those that hold you
and don't ask you to explain
that love you through the highs and lows,
the joys, the mess, the pain

and just ignore the ones who tell you
that you shouldn't cry
because crying like a baby
is a sign that you're alive

REQUEST:

Healing from trauma

INTO THE LIGHT

you know how when it's dark
and then someone turns on the light
you have to turn away, bury your head
or shield your eyes?

it's like when you've been freezing
and you step into the warmth
how your skin begins to tingle
like it's slowly being scorched

well, some have lived through nights of ice
through blizzards cold and stark
and some were raised in ways where days
were smothered by the dark

and if you're used to icy darkness
then you fear the sun
and all the fiery light she shines
just makes you want to run

you're terrified she'll blind you
that her rays will pierce you through
and though your heart is broken
you are scared she'll burn that too

see, when the shadows are your friends
and family is the storm
it's easy to believe
the enemy is bright and warm

but let your eyes adjust a little
trust yourself to face her
she will not blind or burn you
and you'll find you can embrace her

no, it will not be easy
flames will lick your open wounds
some days her rays will be so bright
they'll overpower you

but one day you will realise
you've absorbed a little light
and you've regained a spark
that's helped your inner fire ignite

and that is when you'll look back
and see just how far you've come
through cold and darkness, each day
one
    step
       closer
         to the sun

REQUEST:

Postnatal depression

ON THE ROCKS

you looked across the ocean with a creeping sense of dread
and others watched with no clue of the tempest in your head
then as the waves washed over you, they knocked you to the sand
and all the people looking on just couldn't understand

why you couldn't get back up, why you could fight no more
and why you let the tide take hold and wash you to the shore
they thought you didn't care enough, that you had given in
but what they didn't realise was you'd given everything

see, you'd become a lighthouse standing strong upon the rocks
to save the ships from finding themselves broken, stranded, lost
you watched over the ships at sea each moment of each day
'til you became quite terrified and nervous of the waves

you brightly lit the way but the sea consumed your shine
and then you stood in darkness in the shadows left behind
you called across the ocean so the ships knew you were there
but your voice became a whisper and was swallowed by the air

your days became exhausting, you were vulnerable and scared
so when the stormy weather came you had no strength to spare
you surrendered to the darkness and you crumbled and you fell,
your light had ceased its shining and you couldn't cry for help

but in amongst the ships there were some lifeboats that deployed
'cause though your light was out they knew it hadn't been destroyed
they picked up all your pieces and together you rebuilt
and you learned to free yourself from feeling failure and guilt

and now you watch the ocean from its surf down to its floor
even braver, more resilient and stronger than before
and though it's not plain sailing every minute of each day,
you're now no longer terrified and anxious of the waves

and even when it's stormy now, you know you'll make it through
just as long as you are sure to save
a little light for you

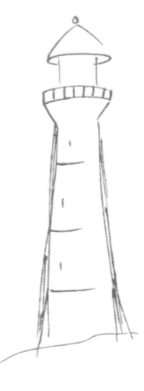

SABOTAGE

let me introduce you
to a woman that I know
she hears my every thought
and follows everywhere I go

she wakes me up abruptly sometimes
when I'm fast asleep
and keeps me up for hours
whilst she taunts and laughs at me

she takes joy in convincing me
that I am hard to love
that if I'm less than perfect
then I'll never be enough

she battles with my confidence
and wrestles with my pride
she's like a double agent
but she's never on my side

she knows just how to sabotage
by sowing seeds of doubt
and arguing with logic
in a voice that likes to shout

and you'd think I wouldn't listen
that I'd turn and walk away
but it's so hard to ignore her
when she knows just what to say

in a way that makes me question
things I've thought and done and said,
you see, she is an imposter
and she lives inside my head

MAN UP

man up, man up, man up they say
'cause real men never cry
they're uncomfortable with feelings
so just tell them that you're fine

swallow down your sorrow
for it's hard for them to hear
yes, I know it tastes like poison
but they cannot bear your tears

but sorrow can't be swallowed
see, it catches in the throat
and it blocks up all the airways
'cause there's nowhere it can go

so then they're left with silence
and they'll say they never knew
that you were choking, but in secret
some of them are choking too

but they're afraid to say so
and too scared to ask for help
in case they're told they're not real men
like everybody else

man up, man up, man up they say
but silence can be loud
and if they're not careful, it might
scream

MAN DOWN
MAN DOWN
MAN DOWN

SMALL MINDS

you tell her it isn't that serious
that she should just laugh, crack a smile
she should lighten up
'cause her tears are too much
can't she take a joke once in a while?

you tell her that it's no big deal
and she should just brush it aside and move on
and if that's too hard
and she takes it to heart
then it's her that must be in the wrong

you tell her she's making a mountain
out of something the size of a mound
that she's made it far more
than it had been before -
she should really be playing it down

but maybe it's all just a cover
'cause you've not even bothered to try
to listen, respect,
understand not deflect
all the things she is saying and why

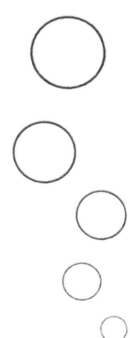

and maybe you can't see the mountain
'cause there isn't the room in your mind
so you only think small,
question nothing at all
'cause you're scared of the answers you'll find

see, it takes far less effort to blame her
than to challenge the thoughts in your head
so you tell her it isn't that deep, but perhaps
you are simply just out of your depth

STICKS AND STONES

sticks and stones may break my bones
but words will cut me deep
they'll keep on hurting long after
the breaks and bruises heal

you see, the sticks will meet my skin,
the stones may hit my bones
but words will carve their way beneath
and make my soul their home

and this gives them the power
to control me and to win
'cause now I've words of worthlessness
from outside and within

see stones are thrown in anger
but our words are thrown in spite
and whilst they're easier to pitch
they're more difficult to fight

because we cannot run away,
we cannot just unhear them,
because their echoes resonate
long after we are near them

and if we are not careful
then those words become our voice
one that learns to shout the loudest
and to make the biggest noise

so do not be the reason
someone hates their own reflection
or thinks they are not worthy
or deserving of affection

and when you pick your words
weigh them awhile between your palms
consider whether hurling them
will heal or hurt or harm

yes, sticks and stones may break a bone
but words can break a heart
and they can be the reason
someone tears themself apart

so if you wouldn't break their bones
by throwing stones and sticks
it's likely for the best
that some words do not leave your lips

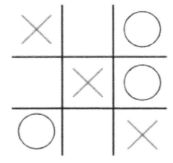

SOMEONE

she was walking home
she was just going for a run
she was someone's daughter,
someone's sister, someone's mum

that's the way we tell it
in the hope that someone sees
that this could be someone they love
that 'she' could have been 'me'

and maybe we say things like this
to give ourselves a shock
to remind us this world's not as kind
as we once thought it was

see, I will always have to think
about the routes I walk
about the clothes I choose to wear
and the way I wish to talk

but I am not defined
by all the roles I hold in life
I don't just matter 'cause I'm
someone's mother, someone's wife

and we shouldn't need to reference
the people we hold dear
just to gather empathy
for those no longer here

yes, she was out running,
she was walking home one day
but she doesn't need conditions
and we shouldn't need to say

that she was someone's daughter,
someone's sister, someone's mom
it should be quite enough
to simply say

she was someone

For Uncle Paul

****

In memory of Auntie Kris

LITTLE THINGS

the cup that's by the bedside
that first good morning kiss
the car journeys together -
these are the things I miss

holding your hand whilst walking
the smell of your perfume
the shoes still on the doormat
as if you'll come home soon

and people say "remember
all the great times that you shared"
but they don't fill the empty spaces
left now you're not there

see, all those empty spaces
were not left by something big
they're left by all the tiny little ways
we used to live

and I know there will come a day
when it won't be so hard
to walk without you there
or drive without you in the car

but for now, I cannot move the cup
I cannot move the shoes
'cause all these little things of yours
are helping me get through

so I will keep them close
and I'll hold on a little longer
until I know I'm ready
and I feel a little stronger

see, all your little things
are helping fill this empty space
and I know one day I'll move them
but today is not that day

REQUEST:

Domestic abuse/violence

WAR OF THE WAVES

I met you on the island
when you walked into the bar
and I very quickly noticed
the tattoo upon your arm

you told me how you got it –
an adventure on the waves
that had quickly turned to peril
when you'd become a pirate slave

they marked you with their crossbones
and a skull that sat above
that would watch you like a shadow
and tell you you weren't enough

they thought because they'd branded you
that you would never leave
but you gathered strength and spirit,
just enough to set you free

you swam and swam for miles
until you reached the island's edge
then you ran and ran much further
until you felt it safe to rest

the journey was exhausting
and you tell me, though you're free
that you're lost and you are broken
but I'll tell you what I see

the shadows that you carry
and the mark upon your arm
are all lingering reminders
of the wounds across your heart

and you're left with broken pieces
like a puzzle to be solved
but although they broke your spirit
they will never break your soul

see you've faced so many battles
but you've finally won the war
for you refuse to let them hurt you
and control you anymore

so whilst you won't forget the seas
that left you with that mark
it's a mark of strength and triumph -
every warrior has scars

REQUEST:

To comfort someone with stage 4 cancer and bipolar

THE RAINBOW

you walk along your rainbow
like a tightrope in the sky
on one side there are dark clouds,
on the other there's sunshine

it often feels a balance
between the brightness and the grey
and it's a heavy and exhausting feat
to walk it every day

but one day on your rainbow,
you spy a pot of gold
and it shimmers in the sunlight
like a treasure to behold

and as you wander closer then
and open up the pot,
you realise that it's filled with riches
you've already got

for out of it floats memories
of all the times you've laughed
and you're soon surrounded by
the happy moments of your past

then stardust and their heartbeats
gather round and hover near
they're all the lives you've touched
and all the people you hold dear

and your rainbow stretches onward
but it isn't time to cross
so you sit and rest awhile
with all the riches from your pot

and your technicolour tightrope
feels a little less unsteady
and your loved ones and your laughter
make the journey far less heavy

and though storm clouds will linger
turning brighter days to dark,
just hang onto that rainbow
in its multicoloured arc

and let it all remind you
when the days feel dark and cold
that we need a little rain
if we're to reach our pot of gold

REQUEST:

Schizophrenia

REALITY TV

it's quiet in the house and there's no one else around
but somewhere up the stairs he thinks he hears a distant sound
so he follows where it leads and climbs the ladder to the attic
and the noise explodes as suddenly his brain is filled with static

see over in the corner, a tv flickers bright
and it plays a programme he knows well - the story of his life
the next episode is starting as he watches from the door
and a dark song starts playing as shapes dance along the walls

and as just then he sees himself appear upon the screen,
he knows it's not, but feels so sure this episode is real
he's running down a pathway and the trees are closing in
he knows people are following - he hears them whispering

it's at that point he feels as if he's losing all control
and he stumbles and he spirals down a giant rabbit hole
and as he tumbles all the trees start shrinking 'til they're small
and the toadstools underneath them are now standing six feet tall

and underneath the toadstools there are people sheltering
but their faces are like shadows and he feels them watching him
so he turns himself away and finds behind him there's a lake
and he looks into the water but can't recognize his face

he feels just like a ghost as if he's all but disappeared
and he wants to ask the shadows if they really see him here
so he turns around and braces for the faces he will see
but he's back inside the attic and there's nothing on tv

the static has been silenced, the tv has been turned off
and no more faces watch him, no more shadows in the loft
and as he sits exhausted with the lifeless, old tv
he's no energy for anything except staring at the screen
and yet, there's always fear that won't stop knocking at his heart
for he never can be sure when his next episode will start

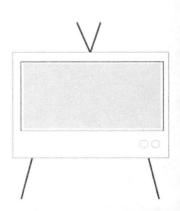

I'M FINE

today I said, "I'm fine" not once
but five times altogether
when people asked, "how are you?"
then made small talk of the weather

and so I hid behind my mask,
the one I'd worn a while
I set in place my bravest face
and dressed it with a smile

and that was how the day went
all "I'm fine" and talk of rain
until somebody asked me how I was –
then asked again

they asked if I was truly fine
and I said I was not
and they said they were sorry
that they couldn't do a lot

but then they sat beside me
whilst I spoke the truth at last
they listened and they held me
when the tears broke through my mask

and where before I'd felt I should
maintain this brave façade,
I realised there was much to gain
by letting down my guard

see, though my load was still the same
it now was not as heavy
'cause sitting and offloading some
had helped a bit already

today they asked, "how are you?"
and I told them I was fine
'til someone saw behind the mask
and asked me one more time

and though they may have felt
that there was little they could do
they'll never know how much it meant
to tell someone the truth

REQUEST:

Borderline personality disorder

TUG 'O' WAR

she feels so many things at once
they're all creating tension
like she's playing tug 'o' war with ropes
that pull in all directions

she clings on to the rope
hoping it cannot get away
but if she holds too tightly
it will stretch and burn and fray

and if the rope gets broken
then she'll give herself the blame
and she'll be consumed by guilt
and then be eaten up by shame

see, everything she feels
she feels right up to the edge
her anger feels as if there's water
boiling in her head

her happiness is flying
like she's soaring through the clouds
and her heart is fierce and roars with love
but sometimes roars too loud

her fear is like a monster
with its hands around her neck
and her panic's like a vacuum
that is stealing every breath

her sadness overwhelms her
like her tears might flood her soul
and though your arms are warm as fire
your silence is freezing cold

so when she craves your contact,
when she cries to have you near
it's because she thinks she's drowning
or because the monster's here

and she'll cling on to you tightly
just as if you were her rope
so coil yourself around her
because it just might help her cope

REQUEST:

Losing a loved one to addiction

DROWNING

he played amongst the waves and put his trust within the surf
but the ocean took him hostage and convinced him of his thirst
you could see that he was drowning, so you tried to rescue him
but he pushed you further under as you tried to help him swim

he scrambled for a faulty raft, a broken, leaky boat
and he surfed the briefest moments where they both kept him afloat
he chased the surf and found that big enough was not enough
until one day the storm came and the waves became too much

it plunged you into darkness, to a null and empty void
and the world just murmured nearby like some haunting background noise
then life grew up around you like a forest of your grief
and at first it was all dark and dense, no sense of light relief

you were surrounded by the shadows of the person he became
and the ifs and maybes made your heart break time and time again
but as the world kept murmuring, its breath created breeze
and the sunlight started creeping through the softly swaying leaves

and though it may be fleeting now, the sun drives out the dark
and your memories and love light up the cracks along your heart
you crave this light and warmth that lets your forest feel at peace,
that changes the shapes the shadows make and reminds your heart to beat

and he knows how you're feeling you see, he was once trapped too
whilst your bars are leaves and branches his were waves stormy and blue
so whilst your forest will remain, and at times you'll still feel trapped
release the ifs and maybes - try to stop them coming back

and allow your love and memories to unlock your cage of trees
and let the sun share warm reminders that he now, at least, is free

SEASONS

we all have an autumn
a time to let go
of things that are no longer
helping us grow

a time to reveal
all the colours we cover
with sunshine and light
in the midst of our summer

a time when our souls
and our spirits prepare
to return to their roots
and to lay themselves bare

and as all our petals
and leaves begin falling,
our breath becomes cooler,
our nights start to draw in,

we realise our winter
is heading this way
with cold that assumes control
over our days

with dark that's determined
to not let us win
to fight with the light
hibernating within

and I know that it's tough,
it's exhausting and hard
to rally your spirit
and soul from the dark

but there'll come a day
when your petals return,
your days become warmer,
the darkness adjourns

so right now, you feel
like your winter won't leave
there's ice getting caught
in your throat as you breathe

but when it feels so bleak
you want to give in
hang in there, remember
we all have a spring

SPRING

new beginnings, discoveries,
breakthroughs, hope, making way,
emerging, progress, trusting,
overcoming

POSSIBILITIES

remember as a child
when you'd walk amongst the trees
and you'd find a stick
that held so many possibilities

it could have been an arrow,
it could've been a sword,
it could've a telescope,
a microphone, an oar

it could've been a hook you used
to catch things from afar
and it could've been a catapult
that launched a shooting star

it could've been a flute that played
a song you knew so well
and it could've been a wand
ready to cast a thousand spells

and now, what if I told you
that the stick was all of these
because there lies a certain sense
of magic in the trees

a magic that reminds us
we are not too old to play
that helps us see the awe
and wonder wrapped in every day

see, the forest is our playground
and the paths between the trees
are endless new beginnings
of adventures to be seized

so grab that stick and row to shore
then search the midnight sky
play your favourite song
then cast a spell that makes you fly

catch a shooting star
and launch it back beyond the clouds
search for hidden gold
and mark an X upon the ground

remember how it feels to live
like you've nothing to lose
when just a simple stick can be
whatever you might choose

then seize those new beginnings
strewn across the forest floor
'cause adventure's out there waiting
so, what are you waiting for?

WHAT IF?

what if the mermaids are all of the women
cast overboard 'cause of old superstition
drowning beneath the waves, gasping for breath
then forging a tail with the strength they have left?

and what if the dragons with their breath ablaze
were once little lizards all thrown to the flames,
choking on smoke and then swallowing flares
then rising up claiming that power as theirs?

and maybe the vampires favour the night
'cause they've been kept in the dark most of their lives
starved of companions, affection and love
'til they have no choice but to feed on our blood

yes, what if these creatures of magic and myth
are those who've known darkness but chosen to live?
chosen to breathe and to rise and survive
to harness adversity hoping they'll thrive?

and what if you too, have been thrown to the waves,
befriended the night and encountered the flames?
and so you've assumed that you're destined to burn,
to drown in the darkness, but what if you learned...

that maybe your story is not over yet
that there are still pages that need to be read?
pages of oceans that you're yet to swim
fiery chapters for you to breathe in
lines built on words that are so full of light
of such warmth and strength, they inspire you to write

so what if you choose now to pick up a pen
and write through the night 'til you come to the end?
and what if you read it back? well, then you'll find
your story has always held magic inside

THE PHOENIX

they can burn your spirit

leaving only charred remains

but from within the debris

like a phoenix from the flames

you will rise again more powerful

and stronger than before

for you know your inner fire

helps you drive away their storm

IN MY SHOES

if I were in your shoes, you say
I wouldn't feel a thing
because those shoes look comfortable
and easy to walk in

if I were in your shoes, you say
I wouldn't walk so far
I'd work smarter not harder
and I'd still be where you are

if I were in your shoes, you say
then I would not complain
we don't get anywhere in life
without a little pain

but you're not in my shoes
'cause if you were, you'd realise
it's not about the shoes as much
as how they feel inside

you see, for years I did not have
such easy, comfy shoes
and working hard to just scrape by
was all that I could do

so go ahead, climb mountains
with nothing on your feet
crawl along through mud
without a thing to keep you clean

wade across the river
with no boots to keep you dry
bare your soles and let them burn
as you run through the fire

and when your toes are bleeding,
when your heels are black and blue,
when your soles are weary,
red and raw and swollen too

yes, when your feet are blistered
and they're caked in blood and dirt
then walk a mile in my shoes
and tell me they don't hurt

THE YES, NO GAME

I bet there is a word you use but often do not mean it
a word that can be heavy and yet hollow when we speak it
a word that's made of just three letters - Y and E and S
and even when our head screams "no!" our mouth still whispers "yes"

but do not use this word just to placate or calm or flatter
do not make the mistake of thinking your voice doesn't matter

see, you don't have to 'yes' your way through meeting after meeting,
accepting and allowing whilst agreeing and agreeing

you don't have to nod 'yes' to everything in conversation
and being who they want you to, is not your obligation

do not be saying 'yes' just 'cause they've told you it's polite
you shouldn't feel scared of what will happen otherwise

'cause 'yes' to someone else may mean the opposite for you
and letting someone win may mean it's you that has to lose

your 'yes' should not be default else there's damage to be done
and it leaves an empty feeling but it's one that weighs a ton

so try to pay attention to the voice inside your head
and listen carefully for words that you can use instead
see, there is one such word you'll hear that holds tremendous power
and if they do not listen, raise your voice and say it louder

say it with your head held high and proudly lift your chin
feel your heart beat faster as the voice inside you sings
and when you do, you'll see you should have done this long ago
'cause you'll have just discovered all the power in your 'no'

PIECES

I watched her drop the mirror
saw her face adopt the fear
that she would now be destined
to bad luck for seven years

but she looked at the pieces
there were hundreds, maybe more
and she noticed how they caught the light
in ways they'd not before

the light was bouncing everywhere
all spirited and bright
a hundred little mirrors
bringing all that light to life

so she picked up all the pieces
whilst she still had every chance
and she turned her bad luck
into opportunities to dance

and if you ever watched her
you would notice how she smiled,
how she moved and shimmered
like her soul had come alive

and if you didn't know her secret
you would not consider
that the glitterball she danced around
was once a broken mirror

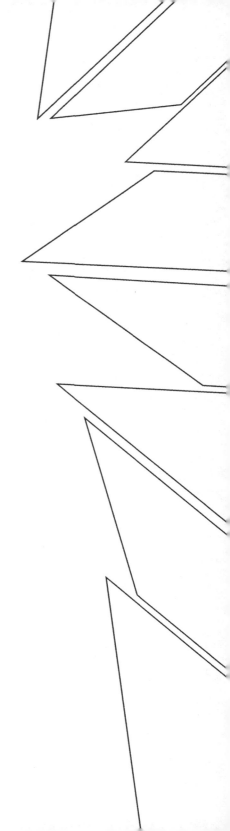

MOTHERS

this is for the mothers
and the ones who soon will be
the ones it hasn't happened for
but want it desperately

this is for the mothers
dearly missed now they are gone
and this is for the mothers
left behind, missing someone

this is for the fathers
who must be a mum as well
and this is for the mothers
doing this all by themselves

this is for the others
standing in and stepping up
for those who wonder every day
if what they do is enough

this is for the mothers
who are giving all they've got
committing every moment
to a role that never stops

and though they do not ask for thanks
they do deserve our praise
for everything they do
that we don't see them do each day

so, this is for the mothers
every single one of us
that have something in common –
we do what we do for love

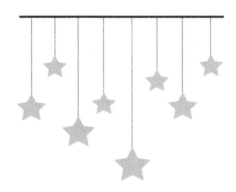

MASQUERADE

she buttoned up her jacket
and she headed to the ball
and hoped her masquerade
would be enough to fool them all

but as she reached the party,
she found herself alone
for the masks had stopped her seeing
who she did and did not know

then amidst a trumpet fanfare
a VIP arrived
she'd heard about this special guest
The Master of Disguise

his outfit was astounding
and he moved with sleight of hand,
he spoke in lots of riddles
that no one could understand

he had an air of mystery
that everybody craved
but when they got too close to him
he moved himself away

and as they tried to follow him
she came to realise,
that they'd never see beyond his mask,
his trickery and lies

and she knew it was the same for her
and everybody there
so she took the mask from off her face
and left it on a chair

and as she did, she noticed
that some others did it too
and she smiled at all the faces
that belonged to those she knew

and now no longer limited
by mystery and masks
they danced upon the tables,
they shared stories and they laughed

and we all do the same
we try disguising what's within
we hide behind a role we've built
in hopes we'll fit right in

and then we work the whole time -
we undo and readjust
we take off our disguises
for the people that we trust

see, we join the masquerade
but then stand wishing all the time
to be recognised for who we are
behind our masked disguise

EARTHQUAKES

some say that if we're gentle
with our children, they won't cope
with all the problems in this
big, bad, tough world as they grow

but have they once considered,
that the ones who make it tough
are the adults who weren't taught
to understand themselves enough?

the adults who, as children
were told 'shut up and sit down'
to be silent and to bury
their emotions in the ground

and that would be the end of it
pretend it never happened
that they never felt frustrated
or felt fearful or felt saddened

well, that's not how emotions work
they fester underneath
and if they are not managed
or acknowledged, they won't leave

the longer they're unmanaged
the more time they have to grow
and if they can't grow outwards
they'll grow deeper than we know

until they reach our core and then
create their own earthquakes
where for a while, the ground is still
but then begins to shake

and then the cracks of anger show –
the fissures full of fear
and we can try ignoring them
but they won't disappear

until all of those buried feelings
one day will explode
and years of sadness, guilt and shame
will have somewhere to go

and go they will to children
who are told 'control yourselves'
by adults who've not learnt to cope
with feeling overwhelmed

so maybe we'll be gentle
and we might just do some good
raising children who will build
a world that's far less tough

and maybe we'll create far fewer
earthquakes than before
and we'll prepare for peace
and stop preparing them for war

For those affected by
the war in Ukraine

CALL TO ARMS

in this world there are arms that hate
that damage and destruct
that rage and wreck and ruin
and that steal the ones we love

these arms are loud and cold and harsh
and powered so by hate
and they delight in seeing people
fall and burn and break

but there are also gentle arms
the ones that hold us tight
that whisper in the softest voice
that things will be alright

they catch us if we're falling
and they help us heal from harm
their warmth provides some solace
from those other vengeful arms

see whilst one tries to break the world
the other keeps it spinning
reminding us to fight hard
for the right to keep on living

and though our arms of empathy
can't change the world alone
they can change little pockets
and they can bring people hope

so let's all wrap our arms
around the pockets we can find
and prove that there are arms out there
determined to be kind

and when it all feels helpless
like our actions aren't enough
just know we'll make a difference
if we all come armed with love

This was not a request, but I wanted to provide some context.

I wrote these next two poems during lockdown for the Covid pandemic. My mother had to shield and so we were all very conscious from early on about keeping our distance. I found it incredibly difficult - as I know so many did – not to be able to see loved ones.

Whilst I know it has not 'retreated' completely, and some of us are still dealing with losses as a result of it all, we are starting to find our way back to some sort of new normal. And what it taught me was that the things we take for granted are often the most important things in our life. As in the poem 'Little Things' earlier in this book, it really is the smallest things that often have the biggest impact on our lives.

xxx

DISARMED

I woke one early morning
and the world all looked the same
but on closer-up inspection
it seemed quite a lot had changed

the world outside my window
had become a foreign land
where I couldn't stand too close to you
and couldn't hold your hand

my kiss was now a bullet
that could kill without a sound
and my heart became a loaded gun
of silent, endless rounds

my hug was now a dagger
razor-sharp and laced with love
and just standing close beside you
was like poison to your lungs

my tools for love and comfort
were now weapons in a war
and we fought a daily battle
like we'd never fought before

and as the war continued
and it seemed we couldn't win
my body was a ticking bomb
of love I held within

my kisses and embraces
were held captive under fear
and they sometimes made a break for it
as anxious, helpless tears

and it felt like near-forever
'til they let our hearts be freed
as our distance forced the enemy
to weaken and retreat

so I revelled in the freedom
to embrace and hold your hand
and as we laid our weapons down
we came to understand

that all the bags and shoes and clothes
we're desperate to buy
the bigger, better house
and all the fancy cars we drive

pale into insignificance
against another's touch
for it turns out what we treasure most
is holding those we love

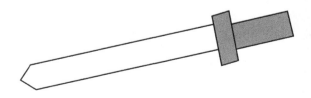

DREAMING

she moaned about the school run like she'd moaned the day before
but she's desperate for the school run now she's stuck behind closed doors

he cursed the 5am alarm that got him out of bed
now he's worried how he'll pay to keep a roof over his head

she hated how they hugged her when she met up with her friends
now she craves their touch because she's been alone for days on end

he complained about the crowded bars - the times he'd queue and wait
now he'd queue and wait for hours just to hang out with his mates

we've grumbled and we've groaned about our easy, normal lives
now we've realised it's normality that helps us feel alive

a cuddle and a coffee in the café up the street
a football match with family that it's safe for us to meet

waiting at the school gates for our children's smiling faces
choosing to stay in or to go out, exploring places

and when life has returned us to our 5am alarms,
the crowded bars, the school run, an embrace in someone's arms

I hope that we can keep in mind the privilege we have
to live with all the freedom that we never knew we had

and I hope we're not complacent and we remember how it was
when the life we took for granted became the life we're dreaming of

RUN FOR YOUR LIFE

there are things I have learned about running
that I think will make brilliant advice
and not just for when running or jogging
but when we're trying to navigate life

like...

how first steps are often the hardest
when you're scared that you'll falter or slow
but if you never choose to get started
then you won't know how far you could go

no...

uphill struggles will not last forever
although sometimes it feels like they will
but I promise that things will get easier
once you can get to the top of the hill

still...

there are times when it feels overwhelming
even when you are trying your best
but when you are weary and cannot go on
then it's ok to slow down and rest

yes...

there will be times you fall by the wayside
but do not be defined by your fall
but by how you rise up so determined
not to let it deter you at all

sure...

there will always be someone who's faster
someone stronger or further in front
but that doesn't negate your achievements
and it doesn't mean you should give up

look...

there's a world full of magic and wonder
round the corner or just down the street
a magic that's found in the skies and the trees
and in all of the people you meet

see...

we are all of us beautiful creatures
capable of much more than we know
if we just take a breath and remember
each step forward is helping us grow

so...

just take the first step and keep breathing
yes, I know that it seems a long way
but for now, simply treasure the journey
and just trust that you'll get there someday

BREAKING THE ROLES

he's decisive, he's determined, so ambitious and assertive
steadfast, unrelenting and he always sticks to plan
passionate when making choices, brave to speak above loud voices
swears and jokes and drinks and smokes 'cause he's a real man

she has a ruthless reputation, has ideas above her station,
wants to climb the ladder but they'd rather watch her fall
she's stubborn and she's far too much, emotional when speaking up
she curses and she drinks, she isn't ladylike at all

she is sweet and she is gentle, empathetic, sentimental
she's the one they turn to for some comfort and advice
'cause she is calm and softly spoken, so in touch with her emotions
always diplomatic, always unassuming, kind

but he is fragile, vulnerable, his tears are quite uncomfortable
he is far too sensitive, he needs to grow a pair
'cause his emotions make him weak, the way he trembles when he speaks,
the way he talks so quietly, you wouldn't know he's there

yes, both of them have family ties but one evades them, one provides
both of them wear suits but only one is power dressing
both have known the ache of loss, the pain that comes from moving on
but one can keep remembering – the other should forget it

they are people, human beings, with the same emotions, feelings
taught that they should show them in completely different ways
taught to neatly fit the mould - to follow rules, assume their roles
but buckle up, 'cause change is coming...

rules are there to break

TIME TO SPEND

imagine if tomorrow
when you got up out of bed
you received one thousand,
one hundred
and forty pounds
to spend

maybe you'd indulge yourself
and buy yourself a treat
or maybe you'd donate a chunk
to those in greater need

maybe you would spend it
on your family and friends
or perhaps you would invest in things
that help you feel content

well now what if I told you
that tomorrow when you wake
you'll be given that exact amount
to go about your day?

but there is just one rule
you see, you cannot save it up
you cannot get it back
and when it's gone, it's gone for good

so be careful how you use it all
before it disappears
don't let yourself regret the way
you spend it whilst it's here

you see, it won't be money
you'll be gifted when you rise
but eleven hundred minutes
so...

how will you spend your time?

A BILLION DREAMS

you know how the night sky holds billions of
stars
burning and shining whenever it's
dark?

well, what if I told you, it's not as it
seems?
that they're actually billions and billions of
dreams

and each, every night when you climb into
bed
the dreams that you have all float out of
your head

up past the trees and then up through the
clouds,
up to the night without making a
sound

they meet with the moon and get ready to
shine
finding their place in the indigo
sky

and that's where they watch, that's where
they wait
until it's their moment, their time and
their place

some stars are tiny and some stars are
huge
see, if the star's big then the dream must be
too

the irony though is that when we are
small
our dreams are the greatest and wildest of
all

then as we get bigger our dreams start to
shrink
our stars begin fading as we
overthink

and there may be times you forget how to
dream
when your mind is busy and struggles to
sleep

and if that does happen, just look to the
sky
look at those stars that are all standing
 by

and search for the dreams all belonging to
you
just biding their time until they can come
true

then blow them a wish and climb up into
bed
pull up the covers and lay down your
head

then close your eyes tightly and promise me
this
never stop dreaming, and always dream
BIG

OUTSIDE THE BOX

don't label yourself as a 'this' or a 'that'
because nouns don't give much room to grow
you see, you're a verb,
a great, big doing word
and there's more you can do than you know

no, you're not a teacher, a pilot, a dancer
'cause what if you want to do more?
to paint and to sing,
create wonderful things
that you've never created before

and maybe you'll dance whilst you're painting
and maybe you'll sing as you fly
but say you're a singer
and they won't consider
searching for you in the sky

the problem is that we are asked when we're small
"well, what will you be when you're grown?"
and we're made to decide
what to do with our lives
when there's so much that we're yet to know

and then the decisions we make from that point
are to lead down the path we have picked
and it's hard to retrace,
redirect and to change
when we've already boxed ourselves in

then we sit in that box with a label
and assume this is where we must stay
so we sit very still
and endure it until
we feel like we might soon suffocate

but you know there's a way to escape it?
lift the lid and then break down the walls
and then step right outside
and perhaps you will find
there's a whole world for you to explore

so when somebody asks, "what do you do?"
do not give them the noun of you work
see, we've all been convinced
that our job is the thing
that defines us our place on this earth

but you're destined for more than a label
and the nouns by which you've been defined
you're a who not a what
and believe it or not
there's so much you could do if you tried

so tear down your closed expectations
and the limits of who you can be
just think outside the box
where it's safe to get lost
'cause you never know where it might lead

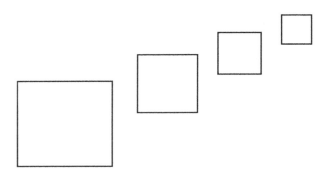

REMEMBER

remember,

when life is hard

and all the days are tough

you have been,

you are

and you will be

enough

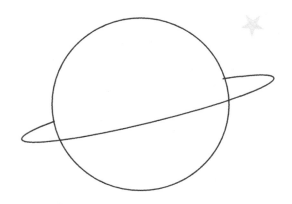

NO MAN'S LAND

when I was young, I had a clock with magic in its hands
and it's taken me 'til recently to really understand

see, when the clock struck thirteen was when things began to change
I was too young for adult life, too old for childhood games
I was in a sort-of limbo where the bar for me was set –
that I should start acting grown-up, but I wasn't grown up yet
so fourteen chimed with sleepovers and gossip after dark
and meeting after school each night with friends down at the park
it chimed with diary entries and with passing notes in class
and buying loads of junk food for a picnic on the grass

then fifteen brought a taste of life's responsibilities
first love, exams, decisions about who I aimed to be
with that came disagreements and arguments with friends
and all the lessons to be learned when things come to an end
but sixteen was a party where we drank our spirits neat
which seemed a good idea until we threw up in the street
it was chatting on a landline phone for hours at a time
and outfits, hair and make-up that I'm glad we left behind

then seventeen got real with us - big choices and heartache
to remind us adulthood was getting closer everyday
but it also brought us freedom - with holidays and cars
and sneaking where we shouldn't be to pubs and clubs and bars
and then the clock struck eighteen and they said 'congratulations'
because to reach that milestone was a cause for celebration
because I'd met the bar they'd set when I was just thirteen
through all the lessons I had learned in all those years between

when I was young, I had a clock with magic in its hands
and it kept me in life's classroom in a sort-of no man's land
on a bridge between two neighbourhoods - to neither I belonged
and I tried to get across whilst putting every third foot wrong
but I think that was the point of it – to fall and make mistakes
to prepare me for the next part of the journey I would take
see that's the thing about what we learn - it cannot be undone
and trying to cross that bridge was tough, but you know what? It was fun!

FLOWER POWER

I'm here to tell the tale
of a garden I once had
where I would watch as Daisy
danced with Poppy in the grass

where Rose lay in her bed
and where Ivy would climb the walls
and sometimes I would listen
to their whispered inner thoughts

see Poppy was the flower
Daisy wished that she could be
a symbol of remembering -
respectful and serene

but Rose looked on as children
plaited Daisy into braids
and wished she could be picked
for all the necklaces they made

yet Poppy watched as Rose grew thorns
that made her strong and tough
a flower fierce and passionate
that people chose for love

and Ivy looked at all of them
and wished she was so bright
she had their greens but not
their yellows, pinks or reds or whites

yet they all looked at Ivy
admiration in their eyes
for even through the cold and frost
she knew how to survive

so Daisy envied Poppy
and Poppy envied Rose
and Rose was jealous of the way
Ivy could grow and grow

and so they all sat focusing
on what they hadn't got
forgetting we are so much more
than everything we're not

see, our power lies in how we all
are different and unique
one flower can be someone's wish
and someone else's weed

so don't compare your petals
to the ones of those next door
don't worry if they tower
whilst you've barely left the floor

yes, you wish you were taller
but perhaps the others dream
of being brave and fearless
the way you've always been

and maybe, though they're way up there
they're always looking down
and wishing they weren't missing
what is happening on the ground

so try not to be jealous
of what someone else can do
because it's very likely
that they're jealous of you too

TAKING FLIGHT

I often like to watch the birds
as they all fly together
strong and persevering
as they navigate all weathers

I've watched them as they're soaring
dancing up against the sky
and I have seen them falter
when they're struggling to fly

I've watched them as they're nesting,
finding food and keeping warm
I've seen them look for shelter
when they sky grows dark with storms

and you are so much like them -
you are strong and brave and smart
but it's not your wings that beat
it's the desires of your heart

and though you have no wings,
believe me, you were born to fly
born to blaze a trail
of who you are across the sky

and know when you are flying high
and soaring through the air
I'll look up and I'll smile with pride
to see you way up there

but if you find it lonely
or you're yearning for your nest
I'll flock and fly beside you
and I'll sit here while you rest

and if the sky grows dark
and if the clouds are building storms,
if you find that you are faltering
I'll catch you as you fall

THE CLOAK

it's almost just a whisper
you can barely hear it there
like tiny strands of stardust
that are floating on the air

blink and you will miss it
like a ghost before your eyes
sheer and so transparent
it will likely pass you by

reach out with your fingers
and you'll hardly feel a thing
as if you're trying to touch the clouds
and gather them all in

but listen and reach out again,
take time to look around
and you will see and feel it
and you'll hear the way it sounds

it echoes in the footsteps
that continue pushing on
it lingers with your words of faith
long after they are gone

it's felt in all the strength you have
that helps you hold on tight
to all those threads of courage
that you cling to every night

it's seen in every rainbow
and in how the day appears
to throw a spear of sunlight
through your deepest, darkest fears

it's hiding in plain sight
though you don't recognise its face
but you can feel its presence
as it offers you embrace

so let it wrap around you
like an almost weightless cloak
and you'll feel a little lighter
once you've dressed yourself in hope

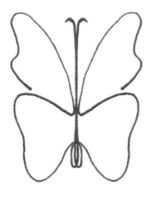

UNDER PRESSURE

mountains can't rise without earthquakes
and rainbows can't form with rain
a match can't ignite 'til you strike it
'cause its friction produces the flame

diamonds are formed under pressure
stars shine brighter when they explode
and volcanoes can't rise from the ashes
until cracks are beginning to show

so I know that you feel like you're breaking
that the rain never seems to subside
that your world has been thoroughly shaken
and you're not sure how you will survive

but when all that pressure keeps building
and you find yourself struggling to breathe
just trust that you're going to get through this
'cause you are a diamond you see

SUMMER

bright, thriving, confidence,
full realisation,
reaping rewards, celebrating,
embracing

For Suki

xxx

THE LETTER BE

let her be confident
let her be brave
let her know beauty
is more than her face

let her be strong
let her know her own mind
and for the most part
let life be too kind

but when it's not
when the days feel tough
let her know she's bolstered
fiercely by love

let her keep dreaming
awake or asleep
let her know feelings
do not make her weak

so let her be gentle
compassionate too
but let her be bold
in her quest for the truth

let the world listen
whenever she speaks
let her move mountains
and dance at their peaks

let her catch galaxies,
comets and stars
let her ride moonbeams
like rockets to Mars

no matter her stature
let her stand tall
and most important
and vital of all

let her be happy
and know her own worth
know that sometimes
she must put herself first

and let her be proud
be determined and free
to be anything
that she chooses to be

beautiful

THERE'S A GIRL

remember the days
when you couldn't stop singing
dancing and dressing up
laughing and grinning?

well, that was before
they all mocked how you dressed
said you would never
fit in with the rest

said that your smile
was the ugliest thing
apart from your dancing
and when you would sing

and so you stopped smiling
and changed what you wore
when music plays
you do not dance anymore

in case you look silly,
in case you feel daft
for fear it will dig up
those memories past

for fear that you'll feel
like you used to back then -
embarrassed and worthless
again and again

see you stopped singing loudly
then stopped altogether,
stopped being someone
that they would remember

but there's a girl watching
she's looking to you
trying to figure out
what she should do

should she stop singing
and swallow her voice?
pick outfits to wear
that would not be her choice?

should she resist urges
to get up and dance?
'cause sitting there quietly
no-one will laugh

but neither will she
she will not know the feeling
of singing so loudly
and dancing so freely

she won't understand
all the power she holds
to do as she chooses
and not as she's told

so warm up your voice
and then strike up the band
pick out your clothes
and get ready to dance

and smile as you do so,
think of that girl
she's the one trapped inside you
so do it for her

SMILE

I'm in the park one afternoon
the skies are dark and grey
and I'm sitting deep in thought
when I hear someone near me say

"cheer up, it might not happen
are you going to smile or not?
you'd be pretty if you smiled"
so I ask him "pretty what?

would I be pretty funny?
or would I be pretty brave?
can my kindness be determined
by the shape my mouth has made?

would I be pretty honest
if I had a pretty grin?
can my resilience be measured
by the curve above my chin?

would I be pretty loyal?
or my spirit pretty wild?
or would I be pretty strong
because I've graced you with a smile?

no, if you want to talk to me
ask what's inside my head
don't focus on the way I look
but how I think instead

see, I'm not ornaments or paintings
that exist to catch your eye
and it's not my job to decorate
or beautify your life

and the sky knows how I'm feeling
'cause he's often told the same
that he's beautiful when sunny
and he's ugly when it rains

but there's magic in his night sky
in the clouds that build his storms
in how his sun sets every night
and then returns at dawn

so you don't think I look pretty?
well, that's none of my concern
'cause who I am behind my smile
determines what I'm worth"

and I think the sky's been listening
'cause he's opened up the clouds
and the park has quickly emptied
and there's no-one else around

and the rain is pretty peaceful
so I sit here with the sky
and the world feels pretty magic
and I smile... 'cause so do I

LISTEN UP

listen up and just pipe down
speak up but don't speak too loud

don't be dull but don't be wild
be fun but don't act a child

age gracefully but don't look old
know your mind but do as you're told

embrace your curves but don't get fat
love yourself but not like that

know your worth but not too much
else they might feel inadequate

wear make-up, look natural though
stand your ground but don't say no

choose the right path, but for who?
right for them or right for you?

right for who they'd rather see
or right for who you'd rather be?

listen up, I'll tell you this
this life of yours is yours to live

so pick the path that's right for you
not the one they tell you to

'cause their obsession with your path
is not your future - it's their past

so don't pipe down and don't speak up
just because they say you should

own your silence, own your wild
own your magic, inner child

'cause if you don't then all their noise
will soon become the loudest voice

and you won't hear the voice within
that says

"you can be anything"

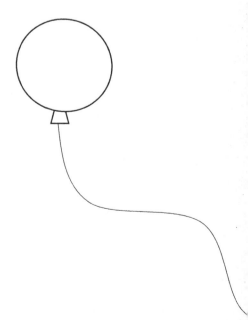

ENGLISH ROSE

she was an English rose they said
with beauty quite unmatched
but when they looked more closely
they were quite taken aback

for they were met with two sides -
fragile petals, wild thorns
half gentleness and daintiness
half hurricanes and storms

but what they didn't realise was
her thorns were only there
to stand as her protection
against those who didn't care

the ones who cut her lifeline
and who tore away her leaves
the ones that thought that she was there
to do with as they pleased

the ones who thought that her job
was just looking beautiful
whilst she dreamt of a purpose
more profound and meaningful

so one day she cried out to them
and let her thorns draw blood
and they cried back that she was not
behaving as she should

that she was just a pretty rose
she had no need for words
she existed for her beauty
to be seen but never heard

so then they clipped her of her thorns
ripped them clean away
stripped her of her armour
of her storms and hurricanes

and then they stood her in a vase
defenceless from attack
see, they loved her silent beauty
but they loathed her fighting back

WRITING HISTORY

when Rosa Parks refused to move
how much did she weigh?
how tall was Rosalind Franklin
when she studied DNA?

when Emmeline Pankhurst died
did people talk about her hair?
and when Amelia Earhart flew
what make-up did she wear?

what size were Mary Seacole's clothes
the day she went to war?
is Marie Curie's face the thing
that she's most famous for?

when Ruby Bridges walked to school,
when Anne Frank wrote her life,
when we watched the constant courage
of Malala Yousafzai

the world was being changed
by every step and every word
by each and every action
that ensured those words were heard

and yes, sometimes the way they looked
was *why* they had to fight –
for freedom, opportunities
and equal human rights

but fight and speak and work they did
to open many doors
that had been inaccessible
and firmly locked before

so when your make-up won't go right
you've had a bad hair day
your clothes all feel a little tight
you hate how much you weigh

remember it can't stop you
having influence, impact
don't let what's on the outside
ever, ever hold you back

you see, there is so much
that you can do behind your looks
just think of all the women
that they write in history books

THE MOON

I took a photo of the moon
when it was full and bright
and it glowed a vivid silver
as it shone against the night

its face I had to capture
in all its beaming glory
but the picture on my camera
told a very different story

see, the photo-moon I saw
was far less silver, far more grey
and where it had been glowing
all the glow had seemed to fade

that perfect circle in the sky
had had its edges blurred
and the moon within the picture
looked a million miles from Earth

and it sort-of got me thinking
about every single time
I'd believed what I had heard -
that the camera never lies

so when I'd seen myself in photos
I had picked out all my flaws
and told myself that these were things
that everybody saw

but when the camera blurs it
or eclipses it from view,
when its glow cannot be captured
then we do not blame the moon

and even with its craters,
when it's covered by the clouds,
when it's barely just a sliver
then we do not talk it down

so let's be like the moon
holding our own amongst the stars
because everybody sees us
as they find us – as we are

and smile for the camera
but don't let it dull your shine
and don't believe the things you hear
'cause the camera often lies

DOMINO EFFECT

you feel so much injustice
and unfairness in your heart
and you know you have to fight it
but it all just feels so hard

like a battle being fought
one side has swords, the other none
or a race being contended
where some must walk whilst others run

like a star that can be touched
if you've a rocket or some wings
but the star's completely out of reach
if you don't have those things

it's mountains you can climb
with views that only some will see
for if you've the wrong equipment
then you'll never reach the peak

and those who choose to fight it
are the strong, the fierce, the brave
for they fight without a sword
and stand with those who walk the race

but picture on that racetrack now
a million dominoes
and you know if just one falters
then the rest are bound to go

so fire up your rockets
sew a thousand pairs of wings
and forge a hundred swords
in faith the underdogs can win

yes, I know it's overwhelming
to try and turn this world around
but pushing just one domino
can knock the whole lot down

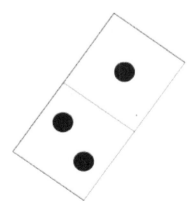

HOW ARE YOU?

"what time will you get in tonight
text me when you're home
be careful if you're driving
or if you're out alone

shout me if you need me
and call me anytime
hey, remember when we did that thing
and laughed until we cried?

take a coat, it's raining
or shelter here with me
let's watch your favourite movie
I've made your favourite tea

I saw this and I thought of you
it really made me smile
just checking in, I hope you're well
I know it's been a while

have some fun at school today
but wear your hat – it's cold
and look, the road's got busy now
so here's my hand to hold"

we always hear and say these things
but rarely do we see
they're just lots of little ways
of saying what we really mean

see, if you listen carefully
you'll hear them everywhere
all the messages of "I love you",
"you're important" and "I care"

THE FLIP SIDE

when we flip a coin
it always lands one of two ways
sometimes it lands on heads
and other times it lands on tails

and people see you like a coin
with sides that are at odds
so what they see's the same
how they interpret it is not

see, when you speak your passions
some will say you've found your voice
whilst others find 'outspoken'
on the flip side of that coin

and if you say you're pretty
some will praise your sense of worth
for others you are arrogant
and praise is undeserved

yes, whilst you share successes
some will share your sense of pride
but for others you'll have landed
on the vain, conceitful side

and when you show ambition
there'll be those that call you brave
and there'll be those that tell you
to stay firmly in your lane

see, if we call out tails
and it lands face-up on heads
we'll flip and flip the coin
until it matches what we've said

but do not let them flip it
so they're up whilst you are down
just speak your mind, hold your head high
change lanes and stand your ground

see, it's not your job to be less
just so they can feel more
and it's not your job to shrink yourself
so they can feel tall

it's not your job to quiet down
so they can make some noise
it's not your job to hide yourself
your strength, your pride, your voice

they've told themselves the side they see
is just the way it is
but the side they see's determined
by the way they feel within

so don't let them choose your value
for what you must understand
is that, like a coin, you're worth something
no matter how you land

SOME BODY

I've teeth that stick out just a little too far
I've marks on my body where I've gathered scars
I've parts of my person that wobble and shake
I've imperfect skin on my imperfect face

my hair's hard to manage - it's coarse and it's thick
I've stripes on my waist, on my belly and hips
I've lines on my forehead and some round my eyes
I've dimples and dents that now live on my thighs

and I used to hide, I got used to concealing
I knew all my angles and how I should breathe in
but all of my scars are the times I've derailed
and got back on track and lived telling the tale

the lines on my forehead and those round my eyes
tell stories of times that I've laughed 'til I cried
and all of the inches and stripes on my hips
are from carrying, growing and birthing my kids

my dimply thighs that all wobble and shake
are the times I've said yes to the chocolate and cake
the times I've decided a moment means more
than hiding and shrinking like I've done before

see I'm happy and healthy and that is what matters
not whether I'm scarred or I'm thinner or fatter
'cause life is a rollercoaster to ride on
it's here for us all to enjoy, not to hide from

it isn't a dress size or holiday snap
but moments in time that we'll never get back
so let's not spend moments that we can't replace
concerned with our bodies, our hair and our face

and let us embrace all the life that we've lived
our bodies are breathing - and that is a gift

Someone requested a follow-up to a poem from my first book called Inside Story about a book that is loved only for the beautiful cover.

The request asked for a Part Two where the book is recognised for what's inside.

INSIDE STORY PART TWO

you saw her in the library
amongst the other books
and the name along her spine
told you to take a closer look

you picked her up and held her
as you took her from the shelf
and you waited patiently
for all the stories she might tell

and she told you of her story
starting 'once upon a time'
and she told you of the towers
she'd been trapped in in her life

she told you of the jealous queens,
the dragons and the trolls
and the time she'd signed her life away
on some enchanted scroll

she spoke about the forests
with the monsters and the wolves
and she told you of the potions
and the poisons and the duels

but then she spoke of one day
when she finally realised
she could control all of the magic
and enchantment in her life

and from that day she needed
no more beanstalks she could climb
and she was no longer waiting
'til a prince came riding by

she now no longer played the part
of vulnerable princess
or the better-seen-but-not-heard
pretty damsel in distress

her words were now empowered
and her chapters spoke of change
and her bravery and kindness
illustrated every page

so when anybody asked you
what it was that she was like
you could tell them she was beautiful
in how she'd lived her life

see, you knew that being beautiful
is more than how we look
and you fell in love forever
with the stories in her book

GREENER

you see their grass is greener
and you wish yours was the same
but yours won't green and yours won't grow
and you take all the blame

but let me tell you something
to relieve this blame you feel
see yes, their grass is greener
but it isn't actually real

INGLISH IZ CONFYOOZING

English is confusing
see, it's so hard to explain
why curd and heard and word and bird
don't look but sound the same

one mouse, two mice, one louse, two lice
one house but it's two houses
and though one spouse is quite enough
we don't say spice but spouses

and how come red can rhyme with said
but bed can't rhyme with paid?
and bear can't rhyme with near
but can be spelled another way?

we can address an envelope
and be enveloped in a dress
and test and rest are just verbs and nouns
but it's not the same for best

if a teacher did it yesterday,
we say that they have taught
but if a preacher gave a sermon
then we don't say they have praught

and why before and four and for
and their and they're and there?
and why's it two and too and to
and wares and wear and where?

yes, English is confusing
with its many spelling patterns
'cause this bit's German, that bit's French
and this part, well that's Latin

so when we look at English
and can distinguish read from read
we should remember we've the world to thank
for this language that we speak

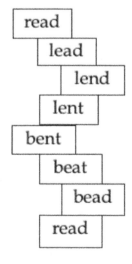

RESISTANCE

there is an army
that you may have met,
you may think you know
but you've seen nothing yet

see, they only rally
and only fight back
when they must defend
'cause they're under attack

otherwise they are
quite gentle and calm
if they're left alone
they've no need to be armed

but just overlook,
disregard their existence
and don't be surprised
when you're met with resistance

'cause all you have seen of them,
all you have heard
is only the tip
of a giant iceberg

you think you see all
but it's only the top
and make no mistake
they are not going to stop

defending their rights
and fighting their fate
knock them down seven times
they'll get up eight

TESTING, TESTING

there are times I've been first and times I've been last
I've aced a distinction, I've just scraped a pass
I've known every answer that's been on a test
I've sat and I've panicked and failed at my desk

I've labelled the countries, I've dated the wars
I've analysed novels and sonnets and more
I've been judged by the margins of numbers and letters,
been told I've done well and that I could do better

but I can say this; that I did not learn less
from failure and fault than I did from success
see, we are much more than the answers we give
'cause it's great and it's grand but it's messy to live
and we learn so much from this everyday test
that isn't included or marked in a test

and when we are gone and they stand up to speak
it won't be of faults but of what we've achieved
and not how we scored in our early exams
but how we were always the first up to dance

the way that we'd sing and the way that we'd cook
with our head in the clouds or our nose in a book
the way that we loved and the way that we cared
the way that they'll miss us when we are not there

and not because we got an A or a D,
a first or a last or a one or a three
but because we were funny, because we were kind
that's how we'll leave love for the ones left behind

so when you sit down and you open that test
yes, read every question and give it your best
but remember, that paper does not define you
so don't give it that power - whatever you do

REQUEST:

A love story between a wolf and rabbit

THE WOLF AND THE RABBIT

the rabbit bounded up the hill,
a full moon in the sky
when she heard the howling of a wolf
which turned into a cry

she bravely climbed the hill
and found a wolf without his pack
crying out in agony,
his legs caught in a trap

and though the rules of nature
told her she should turn and flee
her kindness then resolved her
to ensure that he was freed

so she released each paw from in the trap
then licked his wounds
pretending not to notice
his reaction to the moon

see all the while she'd never stopped
looking into his eyes
for she knew these were the windows
to the soul he'd trapped inside

his eyes were fierce and angry
but she watched them slowly change
through relief to vulnerability
'til only peace remained

and then it was his turn
to quite ignore his nature's laws
to quieten his hungry growl
and put away his claws

"I don't know how you did that,"
were the words he spoke at first
and she looked down to his paws
to check that none of them were hurt

"not that," he said, "I don't know how
you softened me inside"
and then she whispered just three words –
"I see you," she replied

they walked for many hours
counting fireflies and stars
and when the morning sun rose
they were sad they'd have to part

"meet me on the hill," she said,
"the hill on which we met
meet me there this evening
as the sun begins to set"

and both of them considered
whether it was right to meet
were there too many obstacles,
too much adversity?

but they both knew that this
was something they could not ignore
something beyond nature
that they'd never felt before

so they met upon the hill
and as the sun set from above
they proved that there is nothing
quite as powerful as love

DATE NIGHT

I met the moon for coffee
it was Friday night I think
when she watched me hardly sleeping
and invited me for drinks

we found ourselves a table
in the middle of the night
whilst the constellations twinkled
like a thousand fairy lights

she asked me how I'd been
as she poured coffee from a pot
for she said she'd watched me waking up
at midnight quite a lot

I said my head was far too full,
my mind was always on
and when I woke it felt as if
I was the only one

the only one who watched the moon
whilst sitting on my bed
with thoughts that raced at lightning speed
around my busy head

the only one who watched the clock
tick one and two and three
who laid awake and worried
whilst the world was fast asleep

my thoughts remained in orbit
and I couldn't pull them back
as they preferred to swim against
a sky so vast and black

the moon said simply nothing
but she opened up a book
and I saw it was a diary
so I took a closer look

and listed there were names of people
all around the Earth
and all the thoughts and worries
that the moon had overheard

just then my eyes were drawn towards
the name that was my own
and that was when the moon said
"see, you shouldn't feel alone"

and then she pulled me close
using the night sky as a blanket
and said "I know you sometimes feel
so lonely on this planet

but when you cannot sleep, get up
and watch me from your room
and you'll see so many others
having coffee with the moon"

THE BEACH

she stood beneath the moonlight
and she heard a whispered sound
a gentle indication it was here
her soul was found

she looked ahead and saw
the sea reflect a thousand stars
and the waves returned relentlessly
to lift her heavy heart

she'd been a little broken
and she'd been a little lost
but she'd pieced herself together
back to who she knew she was

and as she watched the water
she knew fate had led her there
waiting under stardust
as her heart hung in the air

and then she turned and saw him
he was standing on the sand
and she saw into the future
as she gazed upon this man

he didn't say a thing at first,
he didn't make a sound
for their eyes were busy recognising
everything they'd found

then he broke the steady quiet
with a soft and gentle tone
when he told her that he knew his heart
had finally found its home

and his voice sounded familiar
and she realised it was he
who had whispered in the moonlight
that their souls were meant to be

UNSTOPPABLE

today you are stubborn,
my patience is thin
today you'll persist
until I will give in

today you are willful
you're strong and you're bold
today you'll refuse to do
things you are told

today you will follow
wherever I go
today you will scream
when my answer is no

today you are fierce
and today you are wild
today you'll remind me
that you are a child

today every minute
will seem to last hours
but over the years
I will realise your power

I'll realise your stubbornness
means you're determined
and I'll admire how you have
learnt to stand firm and

how you know when
to sit down or step up
so full of conviction,
self-worth and self-trust

so today you'll be stubborn
today you'll be fierce
today you'll have spirit
that must persevere

today you're determined
today you'll be loud
but tomorrow you'll lead
from the front of the crowd

and where once you were wild
I want you to stay
I don't want you quietened,
silenced or tamed

'cause yesterday's bold
will soon one day I'm sure
be a force that our world
has not known of before

and today you will talk
of the impossible
but tomorrow I know -
you'll be unstoppable

BODIES

we are every body
that they once would try to drown
but we're standing up and speaking up
they cannot keep us down

they thought trying our silence
would be our Achilles' heel
but we'll shout a little louder
so our lips cannot be sealed

we'll tell them of our truth
and then they'll tell us we are wrong
and they'll say we're spitting venom
when we cannot bite our tongues

things get a little heated
when we dance among the flames
and if the world starts burning
we'll be shouldered with the blame

see, they say playing with fire
means you'll get your fingers burnt
but the risk of feeling sparks
is worth the risk of getting hurt

so run your fingers down our spines
and hear it strike a chord
like a sleek, seductive siren
who will lure you from the shore

then stand upon the edge with us
where we've stars in our eyes
and feel exhilarated
when we take a leap and fly

see they cannot tame our spirits
'cause we know how much we're worth
yet if we deign to tell them
then they'll say we've got a nerve

but we're magic and we're moonlight
and we're worth our weight in gold
and they've underestimated
the rebellion in our souls

This poem was written for the England Lionesses – the women's football (soccer) team - before a European tournament.

I think it can apply to so many instances, but knowing the context explains the inclusion of all the football-related words.

THE PRIDE

bring out the banners 'cause now is the time
to harness the fierceness and strength in our pride

because for too long we have been overlooked,
been told we're no match, that we're not good enough

see, some people argue that we are worth less
but we know that they're simply scared of progress

'cause we are not less than and we are not scared
we know all too well it's a jungle out there

and slowly but surely we're making our mark
we'll do extra time just to get to the start

so those that come next don't have so far to run
or so much to tackle or to overcome

so those that look up to us don't get brought down
don't get their dreams dashed or their goals disallowed

we'll keep on campaigning to settle the score
defending positions we've had to fight for

and we're proud of the times that we swam 'gainst the tide
and when they talk us down, we'll continue to rise

and we'll prove their doubt only pushes us more
so watch us move forward and hear how we roar

FAIRYTALE

this is for the princess
who is trapped up in the tower
you think you have no cards to play
no leverage or power

because you've read the books that start
with 'once upon a time'
and so you're waiting
'til a handsome prince comes riding by

you're hoping that your beauty
is enough to see you through
that he will see a pretty face
and fall in love with you

well, let me tell a secret
you see, I once thought like this
I thought that thin or pretty
would deliver true love's kiss

so I craved a certain number
in the clothes that I would wear
I modified my make-up
and the way I wore my hair

but it's not quite as simple
as they make out in the books
true love is not determined
by our bodies or our looks

you see, your real beauty's
not wrapped up in what you weigh
your face may bring you suitors
but it will not make them stay

what will is all your courage
and the way your heart is kind
your spirit, your adventure
and the way you speak your mind

but none of that will matter
until you can see your worth
the truest love you'll ever know
is loving yourself first

so buy your own glass slippers
and take yourself to the ball
then sing and dance as if
nobody else is there at all

let others crave the beauty
that is wrapped within your soul
see, you're waiting to be rescued
just 'cause that's what you've been told

but with your heart and spirit
you don't need anyone else
so let your hair down princess
and go and save yourself

AUTUMN

letting go, change, preparing, slowing down, acceptance, moving on, loss, reflecting

CHANGE

you'd set off on adventure and you'd planned out every path
of everything you'd see and do all laid out on a map

the coves that you'd explore and all the rivers you would cross
the mountains you would climb for stunning views from at the top
the forests you would conquer and the villages you'd find
the things you would discover on the journey of your life

but one day as you reached the river, rain began to pour
and the bridge that you were meant to cross could now be crossed no more
so you decided you would swim as thunder filled the air
but the current dragged you downstream and you ended up elsewhere

you tried to find your path again as you retraced your steps
but when you finally found it there was nothing of it left
and that there is the story of how you've come to be
on a very different course to that of which you'd always dreamed

see there are places on the map that now you'll never reach
journeys you won't take and people you will never meet
coves you can't explore and mountains you will never climb
forests gone forever, villages you'll never find

but there are many roads that times before you might have missed
and there are many places you would not have visited
people you would not have met, sights you would not have viewed,
your path has changed but it still holds adventures made for you

so try to trust the moment and embrace the little things
the smile of a stranger or the sun upon your skin
carve out brand new paths and make new memories with new friends
chase each vivid rainbow and find treasure at the end

and if you're feeling overwhelmed just know that it's ok -
it's hard to trust a journey when you'd planned another way
but if you feel a little lost, consult your map and rest
I know your path looks different now, but your journey's not done yet

THE POWER OF ONE

one leaf can disrupt a whole army of ants
and can leave them all scared and confused
and it takes just one word, even one from a stranger
to render our self-esteem bruised

it takes just one flick of a switch in a light room
to promptly turn everything black
and it only takes one hand to push us too far
just one straw to break our camel's back

it takes just a moment when all is aligned
for the sunshine to blot out the moon
and it takes just one foot to kick us whilst we're down
just one sprinkle of salt in the wound

and yet when we think of ourselves as the one
then we think we've no power at all
that we won't make a difference when this world's so big
and we feel so incredibly small

but it takes just one leaf to announce spring is coming
one seed for a flower to grow
and it takes just one hand to stop someone from falling
which might mean far more than you know

it takes just a word to make somebody's day
just one switch to turn dark into light
and it takes just one foot to stand up for someone,
just one sunrise to soften the night

so harness the power of one for yourself
it's a power you've held all along
yes, I know that you think you can't change the whole world
but you can change the world for someone

THE THIEF

I'll tell you of the time I met
a thief of happy thoughts
he snuck inside my head one night
and cut my thinking short

see I had looked at others
and desired what I lacked
and I'd defined my happiness
by what those others had

their grass looked always greener
though it never seemed to rain
and I thought their sun shone always,
that their winter never came

so the night-thief stole my sunshine
and he took my cloudy skies
he stole my changing seasons
so, of course my grass would die

and what the thief explained then
as self-pity wiped my smile
was that jealousy and happiness
cannot live side-by-side

that if I was so focused
on the lives that others led
I'd be left with only bitter thoughts
and envy in my head

with that he taught me gratitude
and mostly I have learned
for when I lose perspective
then he threatens to return

and that is when I hear
the distant echoes of his voice
that whisper "I'm Comparison
I've come to steal your joy"

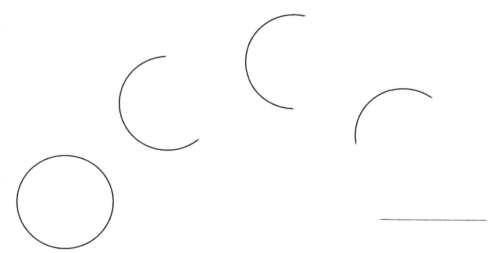

PERFECTION

they make you feel broken
so there's something they can fix
they'll tell you that you're fat
so they can sell you dreams of thin

they'll steer you to bad habits
then they'll offer you their help
then sell you twenty gadgets
so that you can help yourself

they'll try to bring you down
just so that they can lift you up
and they'll make you feel bad
so that you'll pay to feel good

then they'll indulge your spending
so that they can help you save
they'll charge you to stop wanting
all the things they made you crave

they'll trap you 'til you ask
how to escape the daily grind
and you'll pay to move on forwards
when they've told you you're behind

they'll make you feel empty
so you'll pay to feel whole
and they'll make you doubt your inner self
then sell you back your soul

they'll hook you with a promise
that they cannot quite promote
'cause they hold contentment hostage
then they send a ransom note

so pay no mind to them
and all the things they try to fix
and stop striving for perfection
'cause it simply can't exist

WEB OF WORRY

your worry's like a fly
that you have trapped within your web
caught up in the whispers
that you've woven in your head

it buzzes in your brain
with things that happened in the past
like an uninvited visitor
that won't stop coming back

it re-threads all your thoughts
and puts them promptly out of place
so that your web is tied in knots
that won't let you escape

but see, the fly had only meant
to stay a day or two
but you took and held it captive
'til it held you captive too

and now you're in a tug of war
where someone must give in
it's deadlock and it's stalemate
and only one can win

so cut your woven whispers
sever ties you do not need,
thread a different thought process
and grant the fly release

you see, it's only buzzing
'cause its wings just want to fly
so free it from your tangled web
and bid it your goodbye

NOT

you're clinging so tightly
to what you have got
I know that you think that it's love
but it's not

'cause love won't manipulate,
blackmail or bribe
it won't make you think
there is something to hide

see love is not messages
written in code
it's not feeling like
you're an object they own

it won't call you names
it won't trip you with guilt
it will not belittle
the dreams you have built

love won't leave you fearful
of what they'll do next
it won't make you play down
your every success

but it will make you strong
and it will keep you safe
the things that you feel
will all fall into place

no, it won't be perfect
some days will be hard
but love offers glimmers
of light in the dark

because it is patient
because it is calm
love will not hurt you
or bring you to harm

so if you are scared,
if you're made to feel small,
if you have a list
of the names you've been called

if you've been convinced
that you're just not enough
then try and let go
because that isn't love

THE GLASS

the glass was half-empty he argued,
the glass was half-full she had said
so they told him he was pessimistic
that he should think like her instead

but what they had failed to fathom
and what they had struggled to see
was that the state of the glass in the first place
was key to how it was perceived

see her glass had been empty to start with
so of course it was now filling up
whilst his had been full to the brim, overflowing
and spilling right over the cup

so, yes it was now looking emptier
and maybe that loss made him sad
but they told him he couldn't bemoan it
for he had more than some people had

yet for her they did not use this notion
that the way she felt should be ignored
no, they didn't tell her that she couldn't be happy
'cause there would be someone with more

yes, we should count all our blessings
and try to look on the bright side
but a loss is a loss, if we see it or not
so it's easier just to be kind

see they say don't judge books by their covers
well, we shouldn't judge glasses by halves
and we shouldn't judge people if we've no idea
what they had in their glass at the start

THE A Bee C

dot the Is and cross the Ts
mind your Ps and Qs
tell me things from A to Z
between just me and U

and maybe we would notice
that there are so many letters
perhaps we could lose one or two
to make the story better?

but do we take for granted
all the letters that we use?
and how would we decide which ones
we were prepared to lose?

see, if we lost the Z
we would assume it's not that bad
whilst all the bees would mourn it
'cause the zzzzzzz is all they have

but would they cease existing
if we took away the B?
along with ocean creatures
if we took away the C

and how would we express ourselves
if we could not use I?
how would we get the answers
if we couldn't question Y?

would we agree to less
if we were rid of O and K?
and how would we profess our love
if U was stripped away?

how would we all wait our turn
if Qs had disappeared?
and would we all drink coffee
if T was no longer here?

now maybe you are not in love,
you hate the taste of tea,
you don't like asking questions
and you're terrified of bees

and yet, for everyone you know
this may not be the case
the things that you have been through
are not always commonplace

so it is not for us
to dictate everybody's loss
based on whether we can
easily afford the cost

no, let's not take away the Z
and strip it back to A
let's not take away the chance
to ask R U OK?

see, we think it won't affect us -
we'll survive it all unscathed
but life is made of ripples
that can quickly turn to waves

and we think that losing Z
is just a problem for the bees
but we'll be our own undoing
'cause if they go, so do we

BROKEN AND BRUISED

if a tree falls in the forest
and nobody hears it fall
they say that we could question
if it really fell at all

yet sometimes we don't see the sun
or feel it on our skin
but we know that it's still shining
and don't question it exists

if we see a tree in winter
we could think it's always bare
but we never doubt that one day
brand new leaves will linger there

and when we see a fire
we don't tell it to be cold
and it can't stop itself burning
just because that's what it's told

yet sometimes people tell us
of the hurt we've made them feel
and it niggles at our conscience
so we tell them it's not real

"you're just over-reacting
there's no need to cry," we'll say
"you're just so oversensitive
it wasn't meant that way"

but though our egos may be bruised
by all the things they've said,
we can't say how they're feeling
'cause we're not inside their head

see, if we're not in the forest
then it's not our place to tell
the tree that's lying broken
that it never actually fell

WHAT I LEARNED

I learned from my mother
that women are strong
that life can be difficult
but we go on

she taught to be soft
on those finding life hard
to help protect those
who've already been scarred

to work when I need to
but otherwise play
that night time's for dreaming
but so is the day

to be gentle with those
who are tough on themselves
to share out my love
but save some for myself

to only apologise
when I am wrong
to know there is always
a place I belong

to trust in my future
and treasure my past
to smash it each time
that the ceiling is glass

to find the lessons
in relationships lost
because some things in life
are not worth what they cost

but what she taught most
about life and of worth
is that it is only
the best I deserve

and maybe your mother
has taught you the same
but if she has not
well, then I'm here today

to say that you too
deserve only the best
to live out the life
that exists in your head

to find your own strength
and to dream and stand tall
to trust you might fly
when you think you could fall

so never stop dreaming
and never give up
and trust me on this;
you are worthy of love

SHINE

yesterday she told you
she'd been beckoned by the moon
that she was to become a star
and would be leaving soon

and like a supernova,
you felt your heart collapse
knowing that the days ahead
would soon become her last

but mop up all your tears and
squeeze them out amongst the clouds
buy her favourite flower seeds
and plant them in the ground

savour every smile of hers
and send them to the sun
paint the sky her favourite pink
as day has just begun

gather all the words she says
and teach the birds her song
so that the world still speaks of her
even when she's gone

so when the sun comes up
you'll know it's her that's smiling down
and when it rains, you'll feel her love
escaping from the clouds

watch her flowers flourish
and listen for the birds
and hear them sing the echoes
of her voice and of her words

look for her in sunrises
in thunderstorms and snow
because she's trying to tell you
she'll be everywhere you go

and when it's dark, look for the stars
and see the way she shines
and realise – though she'll leave –
she'll never really say goodbye

THE LAST TIME

this might be the last time
that you get to hold their hand
or have a conversation
that you both can understand

this might be the last time
that you get to wave goodbye
or hear them as they're laughing
or hold them when they cry

this might be the last time
that you get to celebrate
or call them after work
so you can talk about your day

this might be the last time
before you're set apart
and though the lasts will hurt
the firsts to come will break your heart

the first time you reach out to them
and realise that they're gone
the first time it's your birthday
but the party's missing one

the first time you have dinner
but there sits an empty chair
the first time that you call them
but of course, there's no one there

yes, this might be the last time
because life can be unkind
so take a million photos
that you'll store inside your mind

and wisely pass the time,
make memories that last forever
because this might be the last time
that you have this time together

JUST VISITING

I sat in the hospital yesterday - I was visiting somebody there
she smiled and she slept as I cradled her hand and whilst I was stroking her hair

I watched as the staff showed such kindness to these people they'd only just met
and my thoughts began wandering the hospital whilst I sat at the side of the bed

I remembered how I'd had my babies in a room that was on the fourth floor
and I realised that right at that moment there could be other babies being born

I realised that there would be patients having life-saving treatment somewhere
and that there would be people all heading on home, discharged from the hospital's care

I realised that there would be visitors who were there helping loved ones to cope
and that there would be families waiting on news with hearts full of love and of hope

see, when I had thought about hospitals, I had thought about sickness and pain
but yesterday, as I sat thinking I felt all the love and the life they contain

and I s'pose life's a bit like a hospital - it's a mixture of sadness and smiles
of compassion and trauma, of grief and of hope that all visit us once in a while

and that's when my thoughts wandered backwards to a thing I had heard many times
from the person whose hair I was stroking as she fell asleep with her hand holding mine

see, for years she had wished she was able to just get up and jump to her feet
to be able to dance like she used to before all these wishes were out of her reach

no, tomorrow's not promised to anyone yet we're often just sitting in wait
and it's only when life starts to leave us we realise we may have left living too late

so let's not be left wanting and wishing for our moment to stand up and dance
let's not wait for next year or tomorrow, let's get up and live
whilst we're given the chance

REQUEST:

Grief

SANDCASTLES

it's hard to watch a castle that you love so much fall down,
to watch it crack and crumble and then sink into the ground
you'll cling onto what's left because it hurts to bid farewell
and you'll want to turn the clock back to the days before it fell

but when it's overwhelming and your heart can take no more
allow yourself a walk to where the ocean hugs the shore
and there you will remember how, in all your younger days
you'd build a castle on the beach then watch it wash away

and you will feel a desperate pull to hold on to the sand
but when you pick it up it all will slip from in your hands
and these will be the times that your heart loses all control
when tears flow in the absence of the thing you wish to hold

but cry your tears of grief and pain as you have done before
and watch the ocean as it keeps returning to the shore
and you will see the tide is just a constant ebb and flow
it loves the land too much to truly ever let it go

and if you let your stream of tears collect between your hands
you'll find it easier to build a castle out of sand
now understand that this one too will soon be washed away -
the ocean will collect it in the twilight of the day

but put your trust within the tide to also bring it home
the love that built your castle will be washed in with the foam
you see, we're all a castle and we're rooted on the land
but there will come a day that we all sink into the sand

then we'll become the ocean for the ones we love the most
and we'll be relentless visitors that never leave their coast
we'll let them feel our presence in the washing of the tide
and call to them in gentle waves so they are by our side

we'll watch them build us castles and they'll never see us smile
when we realise we can hold them and their love for just a while
see love is like the waves themselves all powerful and fierce
with strength that's so unmeasured that it always perseveres

and persevere it will because the ocean understands
and it's always there to watch you building castles in the sand

REQUEST:

Pet loss

GOODBYE

they saw you watching over them
as they finally closed their eyes
they smelt your scent as they breathed
in and out for the last time

they heard the way your voice broke
as you told them they were loved
they felt you as you held them
with your gentle, farewell touch

and now they watch each morning
as you pass their empty bed
they watch you lose composure
and they see the tears you shed

they hear you bear the silence
of the footsteps that are gone
that walk across your heart each day
like echoes of a song

they feel the pang of emptiness
you get when you're alone
in moments when you realise
that they're never coming home

but in their darkest moment
you were there to hold them tight
and they just want the same for you
so you can feel alright

so they're sewing you a rainbow,
weaving ribbons through the sky
so they can let you know
that life is good beyond goodbye

so next time it is raining
and the sun appears as well
just feel and look and listen
to what they are trying to tell

they're telling you it's spring there
with its showers and its sun
where there are endless fields for them
to play and stretch and run

they're telling you they sleep upon
the biggest, softest beds
that they have stitched from all the clouds
that float above your head

they're telling you they're not alone
for there are many others
and they've been reunited
with their parents, sisters, brothers

they're showing you their rainbow
so you know they won't forget you
and to tell you they will always be
so happy that they met you

and they're telling you they love you
and though they'll be dearly missed,
not to worry, 'cause it's beautiful
beyond the rainbow bridge

UNFILTERED

filtered sunsets, filtered skies
make pretty, filtered places
filtered skin and filtered eyes
make pretty, filtered faces

softened truths and blurry lines
so no-one knows what's real
we're weaving this world's worth
into its visual appeal

we're filtering our daily lives
and taking out what's raw
thinking we're eradicating
each and every flaw

yet the sun just keeps on setting
she cares not about her face
for she knows it has no bearing
on her power up in space

she knows she's irreplaceable
because of what she does
that her warmth and strength and energy
are not about her looks

and she is not alone
because the sky thinks like this too
he doesn't care if we don't like
his chosen shade of blue

'cause he has electricity
to control and command
and he holds rainbows, clouds
and hurricanes within his hands

and maybe you have warmth
and electricity within
but all your strength and power
is not captured on your skin

so let the sun set peacefully
in all her fiery glory
and let the lines upon your face
tell everyone your story

yes, pretty filtered photos
may look like the perfect dream
but be wary of perfection
'cause it's never what it seems

so let's all lose the filters
let the world just live and breathe
and accept ourselves unfiltered
'cause isn't that the perfect dream?

WILD

you're a wildflower darling
you cannot be tamed
they recognise your beauty
though they do not know your name

you sing a song of sunshine,
befriend butterflies and bees
you dance amongst the grasses
and you sleep beneath the trees

you're bright but unassuming
you are delicate yet tough
you're rooted but you're ready
for when winds of change do come

and they meet you in the forest
and they'll marvel at the way
you remind them of their childhood
and easy, carefree days

so they'll make of you a bracelet
and they'll weave you through their hair
they'll wish upon your petals
and then blow you to the air

and as they watch you fly
they'll wish that they could fly like that
they'll realise that you have a freedom
they have never had

so they'll pick you for a posy
and they'll tie you at the stem
so they can take a little bit of
freedom home with them

but home is where the heart is
and your heart cannot be still
so home for you is not a vase
upon a windowsill

remember, you're a wildflower
born to ride the wind
to plant your roots on new horizons
each and every spring

so don't ignore your wild heart
'cause freedom's what you breathe
see, that is why they love you so
and why you have to leave

THE EAGLE

the baldest of the eagles
is a leader with no crown
who rules across his kingdom
from his perch whilst looking down

his voice is weak and quiet
but he still commands respect
for he's no need to prove his power,
bravery or strength

and when it comes to people too
something I've often found
is that confidence is quiet
insecurity is loud

and those that shout the loudest
often have the most to prove
if you have to say you're powerful
then is it really true?

if all your strength and bravery
must be a massive show,
what happens when the curtain falls
and everyone goes home?

see, if you perch yourself
upon a self-built pedestal
it's probably 'cause inside
you're feeling really rather small

'cause if you held true power
you'd leave others to their choice
your proof would be your actions
not the volume of your voice

your show would not be needed
for your act would be the same
with or without an audience,
a curtain or a stage

so if you find you're shouting,
take a moment to reflect
and you may find you're trying
to convince yourself – not them

and if you're keen to prove yourself
don't shout about it – do it
an eagle won't announce his strength
he'll just rise up and prove it

FEARLESS

you think that he is fragile,
that he's empty like a shell
you think that all the scars he bears
are from the times he fell

you think that he is broken
like a shattered windowpane
you think he's moving back
with every single step he takes

you think that he is soft
because he holds you in his arms
he's gentle and he's warm
and he is restful and he's calm

you think that he is timid
'cause you rarely hear him speak
and you put all this together
and assume that he is weak

but a bullet has a shell you know
and snakes can hold you tight
yes, they can coil around you
'til you're fighting for your life

an arrow is pulled backwards
until it's left to soar
and you can still find calm
right in the middle of a storm

a dragon keeps you warm
but it can also burn you down
and broken glass will cut you
if you fail to look around

so listen very carefully
to what you might be missing
it's quiet as a whisper
like a very distant ticking

you see, a bomb is quiet
'til the moment that it's not
so do not underestimate
what you think makes him soft

because you may see weakness
but beware of your mistake
else you may find you're fighting
against a dragon or a snake

and you may think you'll win
but he is strong and fierce and tough
and he's pretty fearless
if he's forced to prove that
he's enough

REQUEST

A poem about a
soldier's guilt when
returning from service,
having lost fellow
soldiers in the field

TODAY

today I saw a flower -
it reminded me of you
you stood there in the sunshine
with your petals in full bloom

but you were stood alone
there were no flowers of your kind
standing there beside you
for they had been left behind

in fields that you used to share
with them some time ago
when they became your family
whilst you helped each other grow

but there were stormy days ahead
with skies all dark and grey
fields that were torched by lightning,
flooded by the rain

and though they tried to fight it
there were flowers by your side
that had to lay themselves down
so that others could survive

and I know you feel guilty
that you're growing on without them
but they need you to keep going
so that you can talk about them

to keep their hearts alive
to share their stories and their names
you know if you were in their place
that you would want the same

you'd want them to chase sunshine
and to camp beneath the stars
to honour you by living
whilst they kept you in their hearts

so try to stem your sadness
and those guilty tears you shed
'cause they live on within you
in your petals bright and red

yes, today I saw a poppy
it reminded me of you
and every time I see it
I'll be reminded of them too

THE SPIDER AND THE FLY

your words were smooth as silk at first
like gossamer on the air
and you teased them into tales
designed to trap her in your lair

the tales at first were gentle
they were fun and full of light
but they soon were laced with poison
from your sly, deceitful bite

then the gossamer betrayed you
it was thin, transparent too
and your words soon wove themselves
into a fickle, fragile truth

you walked it like a tightrope
and you hung on by a thread
and when she asked you questions
then you spun the words she said

and as the questions mounted
you just couldn't quite keep up
the threads became all tangled
and you became quite stuck

see each new thread you wove
unraveled those already spun
and they trapped you into many knots
that could not be undone

and as the panic settled in
you tried to wriggle out
but that just tied your stories
into double knots of doubt

see you deftly and you swiftly
spun yourself a web of lies
but you got caught up within it
'cause you're the spider...

and the fly

FREE FALL

whenever we are falling
we are taught to understand
our fall will only stop
when we can hit the ground or land

except when it's in love
that we are headed for a fall
and then we're told it's fate –
that we are destined to be caught

and isn't that ideal?
yes, it's wildly romantic
to think the one we're falling for
will soften up our landing

but I have often wondered
what it is we're supposed to do
when the other person cannot catch us
'cause they're falling too

THE SKY

he asked of me why it was raining
he asked was it tears from the sky?
and I replied yes,
that this was the case -
that even the heavens can cry

he asked of me what was the thunder
he said it was hurting his ears
so I explained sometimes,
even the clouds
need to scream so that somebody hears

he asked of me what was the wind
and why was it whirling and swirling around?
and I told him that even
the sky takes deep breaths
when it's trying to calm itself down

but often we keep our tears secret
and we swallow our own cries for help
and we think that it's weak
to be catching our breath
so we don't let our struggles be felt

and yet, if the clouds never emptied,
if the sky never screamed through the storm
it would sit growing
darker and darker until
it was simply no use to us all

so throw all your fears to the wind dear
and toss all your tears to the clouds
and you will discover
the infinite power
the heavens hold over the ground

see, it's normal and natural to struggle
and it's healthy and human to cry
and if anyone questions
your power my darling
just tell them it's matched by the sky

About the Author

Hi I'm Becky!

I have been writing poetry for years now, but only last year did I become brave enough to start sharing it with people (I'd shared it before that but only anonymously or with friends and family – who feel obliged to say they like it regardless!)

I live in Leicestershire, UK with my husband, our two boys and our very old dog – a beagle called Misty. I used to be a primary school teacher and still enjoy delivering poetry writing workshops in schools across the country. I adore dancing and singing along to musical theatre soundtracks at the top of my voice on long car journeys (other passengers don't love this so much). My favourite thing to do is to create memories with the people that mean the most to me and my favourite season is Autumn because it gives me an excuse to wear chunky knits, drink too many take-away cappuccinos and make my house smell of orange and cinnamon. Maybe this is because I'm a very late-August baby and so life began in Autumn for me!

This is my second book. My first book 'Talking to the Wild' is available on Amazon worldwide or on my Etsy store (also available worldwide).

Future projects include more writing (of course), audio books/ audio recordings of both my books, more products (prints, postcards, notebooks, calendars etc), a children's book of the poem 'Breathe', school workshops and the launch of my YouTube channel where I am hoping to have my poems animated.

I am always available through the channels listed at the beginning of the book and this is where there will be updates of any new projects, collaborations etc. Come and say hi!

And finally... THANK YOU for being a part of this incredible journey with me! Your support is beyond appreciated.

Becky x

Made in the USA
Monee, IL
25 January 2024